WITHDRAWN

ESCAPE!

THE ARTIST'S CABIN

SOLVE YOUR WAY OUT!

Kevin Wood

Use your ART skills to ESCAPE!

Gareth Stevens
PUBLISHING

Please visit our website, www.garethstevens.com. For a free color catalog of all our high-quality books, call toll free 1-800-542-2595 or fax 1-877-542-2596.

Cataloging-in-Publication Data
Names: Wood, Kevin.
Title: The artist's cabin: solve your way out! / Kevin Wood.
Description: New York : Gareth Stevens, 2023. | Series: Escape!
Identifiers: ISBN 9781538277171 (pbk.) | ISBN 9781538277195 (library bound) | ISBN 9781538277188 (6 pack) | ISBN 9781538277201 (ebook)
Subjects: LCSH: Puzzles--Juvenile literature. | Problem solving--Juvenile literature. | Logic puzzles--Juvenile literature. | Arts--Juvenile literature.
Classification: LCC GV1493.W663 2023 | DDC 793.73--dc23

Produced for Gareth Stevens Publishing by Alix Wood Books
Designed and Illustrated by Alix Wood
Editor: Eloise Macgregor

Printed in the United States of America

CPSIA compliance information: Batch # CSGS23 For further information contact Gareth Stevens, New York, New York at 1-800-542-2595.

THE ARTIST'S CABIN

OPEN GALLERY

Art and Sculpture EXHIBITION

ADMIT ONE

Once a year, the town's local artists open their studios to the public. What could be nicer than a trip to a local artist's gallery? You can see some beautiful works of art, maybe chat with the artist, and learn how they create their paintings. That'll be a nice relaxing day out . . . or will it?

HOW TO  ESCAPE!

Use your art knowledge to puzzle your way out of the artist's cabin. Solve puzzles to get the codes you need to open a series of locked boxes. Each box contains one shaped key. You will need all the shapes to open the cabin door. All the information you need to solve the puzzles can be found in this book. Clues to puzzles may be on any page, so read the whole book first.

Get stuck? The answers and hints are hidden at the back of this book.

What started out as a fun family trip to visit the local art studio open day has turned a little sour. As soon as you pull the heavy, wooden door shut behind you, you feel uneasy. The place is eerily quiet. All the windows are locked. The only exit appears to be the door you came through, which has now clicked shut. Examining the door, you see a strange lock on it, with 11 oddly-shaped holes.

There is a hurriedly scribbled letter on the floor in front of you.

I really hope someone finds this note. I have to be quick; they are coming for me. They know I saw them steal the painting, so I have to run and hide. They said they will be back to steal more paintings in an hour or so, so get out if you can.

Did you shut the door? I hope not! It needs the 11 shapes to open it again. You'll need to solve all the puzzles to get the shapes. Be quick.

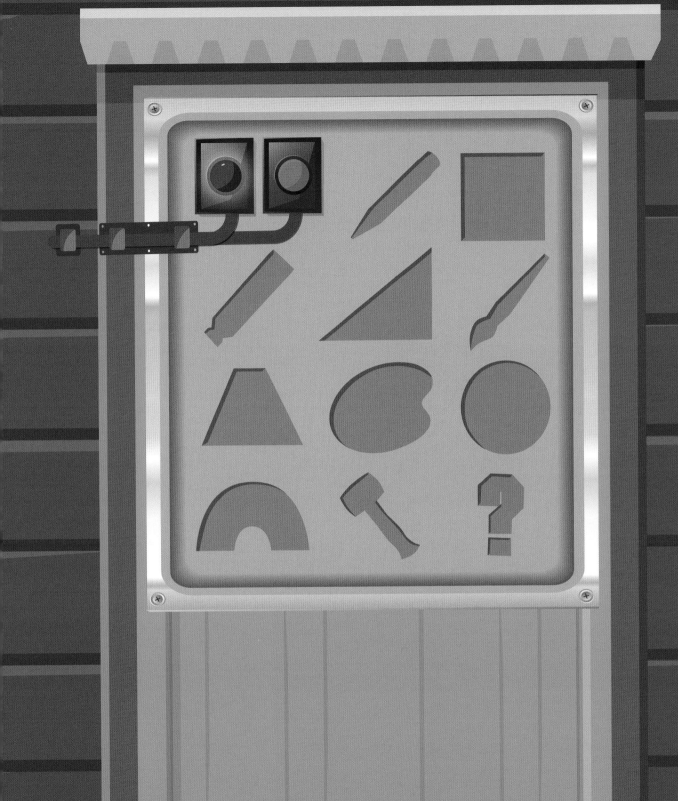

THE ART DESK

It looks as if someone has left the art desk in a hurry. A half-eaten burger and a spilled cup of cold coffee lie on the desk. I wonder what has happened here. At least the pencils look very tidy. There is a tall, round pencil tin on the desk. On its lid is a keypad. Could one of the shapes be in there? It may be easy to open, if only we knew the correct four numbers.

THE GALLERY

As you enter the deserted gallery, you are faced with walls and walls of colorful abstract paintings. There is a strong safe against one wall. Could a shape be in there? If only you knew the four-number combination to open it . . .

Item No: 2

THE STOREROOM

A side door leads to a cold, dark storeroom. You switch on the light and look around. Art supplies fill the shelves. The artist obviously liked to keep everything in order. There is a wooden chest on the floor with a combination lock. You need a four-number code to open it.

Don't forget!
Buy some new
brushes and
Carmine
Gamboge
Ultramarine
Mummia

Item No:
3

11

THE HALL

A large cupboard stands by the hallway stairs. A strange panel on the cupboard has colorful shaped buttons. It seems to be a lock. Perhaps you can press the shapes to open it? But which shapes, and in what order? There are some objects on the hall table . . .

Item No:
8

13

THE HALL TABLE

On the hall table lies a notebook and a locked box. Scraps of paper with notes and designs litter the muddled table.
A, B, C, or D? I don't know!
The notebook is full of facts about art and colors.

Art Notebook

With an artist's work, sometimes you just have to look at it from another perspective.

Pencils

Pencils have either the letter H or the letter B written on them. The letters show how soft or hard the pencil lead is. The softer pencils end with a B. **9B** is the softest. The harder pencils end with an H. **9H** is the hardest. The HB pencil is in the middle. Softer pencils draw nice dark lines.

<u>I usually draw with the soft B pencils.</u>

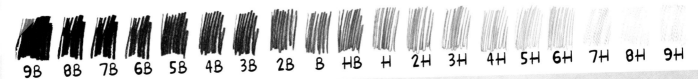

9B 8B 7B 6B 5B 4B 3B 2B B HB H 2H 3H 4H 5H 6H 7H 8H 9H

Light and Dark

The Italian word "chiaroscuro" describes when artists use dramatic light and shade. "Chiaro" means "light" and "scuro" means "dark" in Italian. Artists such as Leonardo da Vinci, Caravaggio, and Rembrandt often used this technique.

chiaro

scuro

scuro

Perhaps I could recreate an image of the stolen painting using a grid? Grids help break a picture up into sections, making it easier to draw. That will help the police know what they are looking for. But I just don't have time...

Paint colors

Colors can have such strange names! Paints might be called after the place they were invented, the substance they are made from, or sometimes after a famous artist who liked to use that paint.

Gamboge is a yellow that got its name from the gamboge tree. It is made from the tree's resin.

Indian Yellow is named after India, the country where it was made. Indian Yellow used to be made from cows' urine! The cows were fed mango leaves to give the urine a bright color.

A brown paint called Mummia used to be made from ground up mummified bodies! It's said artist Edward Burne-Jones buried his mummia paint in his garden when he found out it was made of dead bodies!

Vandyke Brown was named after the Flemish painter Anthony van Dyck, who often used the warm brown color in his paintings.

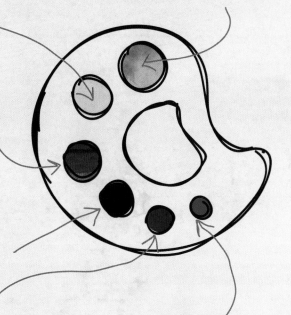

Carmine red is made from crushed beetles! Cochineal insects produce red carminic acid to scare away predators. This red is used in paint and food coloring! I bet I've accidentally eaten some!

Ultramarine blue is a deep blue color, brought to Europe from Afghanistan by ship. Ultramarine means "across the sea."

There is such beautiful art all around the GALLERY. I am FACED with all these amazing colors: the vibrant red, then turn and admire the yellow, turn again and marvel at the pink. And then, in turn, how I love the blue.

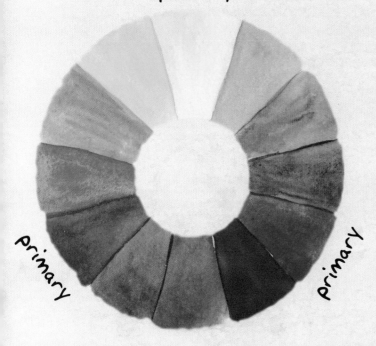

primary

primary

primary

The Color Wheel

The "clock-like" color wheel helps artists choose and mix colors.

Red, blue, and yellow are primary colors. Primary colors can't be made from other colors. Mix the primary colors to make other colors, such as greens, oranges, and purples. If you mix red and blue, you get purple.

Complementary colors

Complementary colors are opposite each other on the color wheel. Red is complementary to green. Complementary colors contrast with each other. If you want something to stand out against its background, paint it in the background's complementary color!

18

Perspective

Perspective is an art technique that gives the appearance of distance or depth of an object. When drawing railroad tracks, you would make the lines get closer together as they disappeared into the distance. You would draw close objects, like these people, larger than the house in the background. The house is actually larger, but because it is in the distance, it appears smaller.

Perspective can also mean the angle or direction in which a person looks at an object. Try looking at things from above, and then at eye level. They will look quite different.

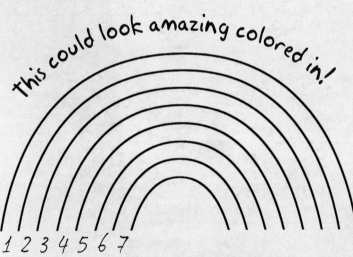

this could look amazing colored in!

1 2 3 4 5 6 7

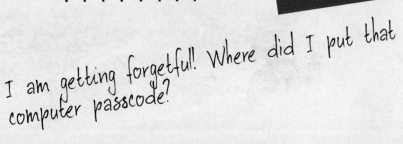

I am getting forgetful! Where did I put that computer passcode?

A Visitor's Guide to the Collection

A painting in the style of Frida Kahlo was donated to the gallery last year. Kahlo was a Mexican painter known for her portraits and self-portraits. Her work was inspired by the plants and nature of Mexico.

Our collection is proud to house several pop art paintings in the style of Andy Warhol. Warhol painted popular subjects such as soup cans and movie stars. He liked printing many copies of the same image and then playing with the colors to create his works of art.

Dutch artist Vincent van Gogh is one of the world's most famous painters. He is well-known for his self-portraits, paintings of sunflowers, and landscapes with starry skies. Many paintings feature cypress trees and swirling colors. A painting in Van Gogh's style can be found in the Collection.

René Magritte was a surrealist painter who liked to paint normal objects in strange places. He often painted men in bowler hats. His paintings often featured pipes, apples, eggs, and cloudy skies.

Pablo Picasso is probably best known for his cubist paintings. Cubists paint an object from different angles in the same picture. For example, a portrait of the side of a face may still feature two eyes. Our collection is pleased to display a copy of a Picasso portrait.

An amateur sketch of a painting by American artist Grant Wood has been given to the gallery. Grant Wood is most famous for his painting *American Gothic*. It features a farming couple standing in front of a building with an arched window.

Surrealist painter Salvador Dalí created paintings about the dreams he had. Surrealism was a style of art where painters created realistic-looking scenes that would be impossible in real life. One of his most famous paintings has images of melting watches!

Looking closely at these works of art can reveal a number of surprises.

UNDER THE BOOK

Tucked under the notebook, next to a locked metal box, you find a quiz.

Art Quiz

1. Which of these artists painted in a Pop Art style?
   a) Vincent Van Gogh b) Salvador Dali c) Andy Warhol

2. Which pencil would make the softest, darkest marks?
   a) 9H b) HB c) 9B d) 2H

3. What does "chiaroscuro" mean?
   a) light and dark b) a landscape c) a shade of blue paint

4. What work of art is the missing stolen painting a copy of?
   a) American Gothic by Grant Wood
   b) Nighthawks by Edward Hopper
   c) The Son of Man by René Magritte

THE DESIGN STUDIO

There is a soft hum coming from the colorful design studio. On the desk is a computer and 3D printer. You could use them to create fantastic art, or maybe even print objects. Could these machines help you unlock the exit door?

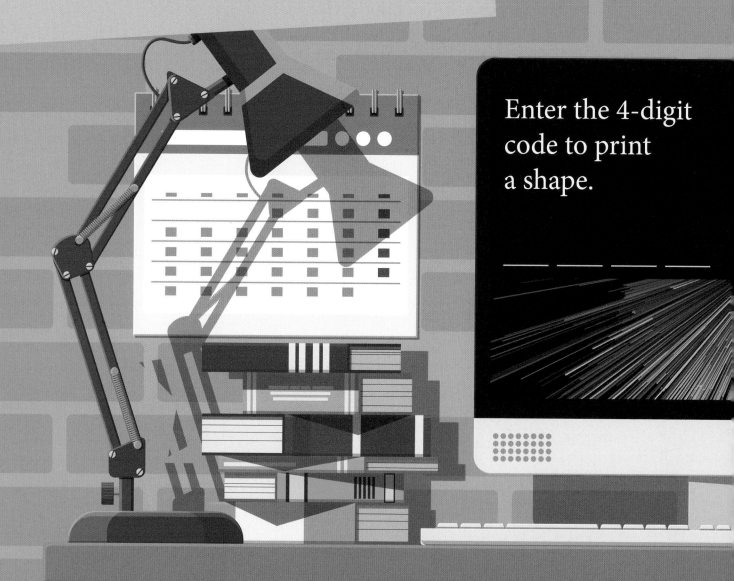

Enter the 4-digit code to print a shape.

____ ____ ____ ____

THE COLLECTION

Back in the hall, a broken door leads to a room full of what appear to be fake art treasures. Could these art copies hold some clues to that safe's combination?

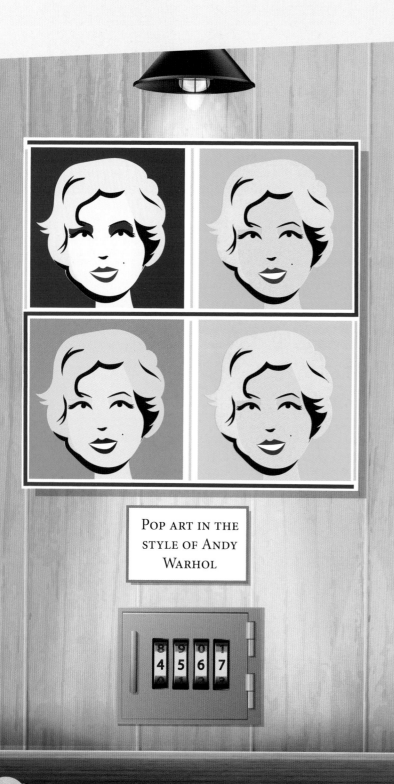

POP ART IN THE STYLE OF ANDY WARHOL

A PORTRAIT IN THE STYLE OF PABLO PICASSO

A FRIDA KAHLO-STYLE PORTRAIT

RENÉ MAGRITTE-
STYLE PAINTING

VINCENT VAN
GOGH-STYLE
"STARRY SKY"

STOLEN ARTWORK!

REWARD FOR
INFORMATION

SALVADOR
DALI-STYLE
SURREALISM

trace me and fill me

Item No: 6

COLOR WHEEL

In an upstairs bedroom, an old suitcase lies on the bed. It is locked, with a three-number combination lock. Was the artist planning a trip? Beside the case is a color wheel. Artists use color wheels to help them choose colors that look good together. The artist had made some notes around the wheel. What could they mean?

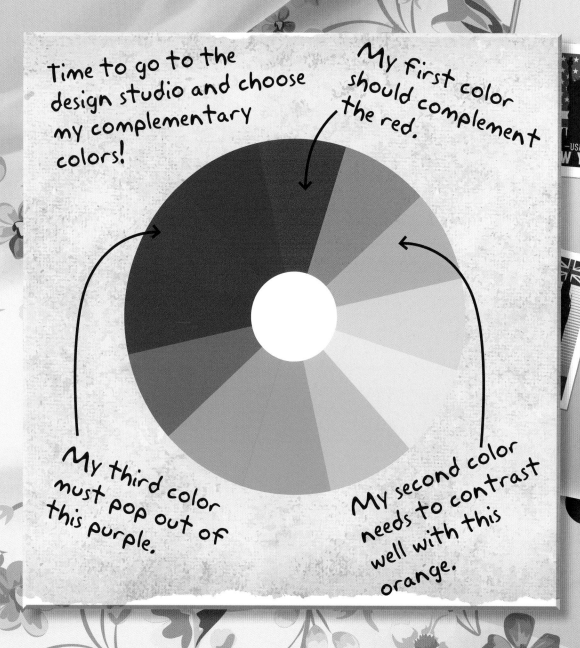

THE GARDEN

Looking out of the locked window you see a beautiful garden. That would inspire any artist! There is a maze decorated with colored flags.
A colorful arched rainbow reminds you of something from a book! Should you solve the maze? Perhaps the flags will help you remember the right way through!

On the wall is a small safe. You'll need a four-digit code to open it. Numbers, not colors? Curious!

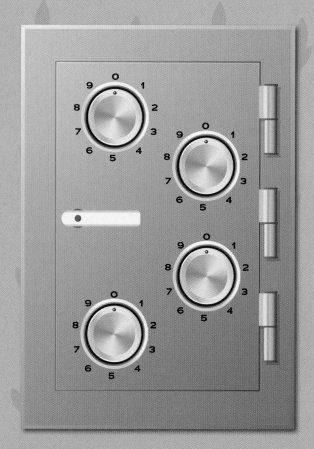

Item No:
4

THE POOL

A sliding glass door leads to an indoor pool where fine marble sculptures are on display. The old statues have been damaged over time but are still quite beautiful. It would be wonderful to restore them. A clothes locker sits poolside.

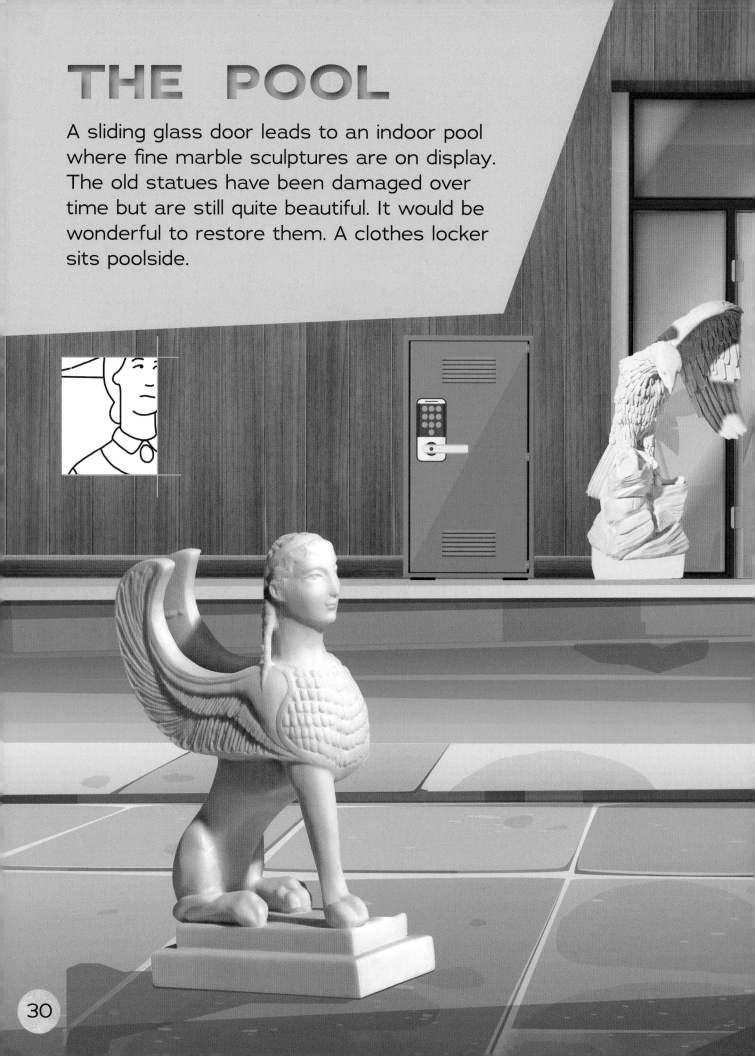

Did you escape the artist's cabin?
Check your answers on page 32.

HINTS

The Art Desk
1. There may be a clue in the notebook?
2. What would an artist put in the tin?
3. The art pencils on the desk look very ordered.

The Gallery
1. Could the answer be right in front of you?
2. Turn and face the paintings.
3. Read the notebook to find a clue to the order.

The Storeroom
1. Is that a shopping list on the wall?
2. What do all the words on the list mean?
3. Link the names with the numbers.

The Hall
1. The shapes on the lock look familiar.
2. Light from a window casts dancing shadows onto the hallway wall.
3. Perhaps there is a clue in the notebook?

The Hall Table
1. The answer and the safe isn't always right in front of you.
2. Have you finished reading the notebook?
3. Bits and pieces of the missing artwork are scattered about the book. Trace the grid on page 16. Then trace the parts to create it.

Under the Book
1. Most of the answers will be close by.
2. Where have you seen a lock that needs A, B, C, or D?
3. Hold the squiggles at eye level.

The Design Studio
1. The numbers you need are right in front of you.
2. You may find a clue in the notebook.
3. Perhaps the artist wrote the code and put it on the shelves?

The Collection
1. Take a close look at those beautiful works of art.
2. A guide might come in handy.
3. The number order is the order in the guide.

Color Wheel
1. Have you seen any information about complementary colors anywhere?
2. Does that color wheel remind you of anything?
3. Have a look in the Design Studio for inspiration.

The Garden
1. Find your way through the maze.
2. What color flags signaled the right way through the maze?
3. Could that rainbow help you?

The Pool
1. It would be great to restore those statues.
2. A number of pieces seem to be scattered around the cabin.
3. Choose your pieces wisely.

ANSWERS A mirror will help you read these answers.

6-7: 2374 [B pencils in position]

8-9: 4723 [numbers in the portrait; instructions on page 18]

10-11: 6752 [paint tube numbers in shopping list order]

12-13: green circle, orange triangle, blue square [chiaroscuro clue on page 16]

14: ccaa [page 21 quiz answers; to answer 4, trace sections of the painting scattered throughout the book onto a grid similar to the one on page 25]

20-21: 9157 [perspective puzzle is on page 14; to read, hold the book at eye level]

22-23: 7234 [numbers in bookshelves; clue page 19]

24-25: 3267 [numbers hidden in the pictures or frames; in page 20 catalog order]

26-27: 684 [complementary colors; numbers taken from the studio clock]

28-29: 2451 [solve the maze; translate the colors to numbers using the rainbow on page 19]

30-31: 6824 [put the numbered statue pieces scattered throughout the book in the right order]